The Magic of Butterflies and Moths

Butterfly and Moth Magic

The Magic of Butterflies and Moths

Butterfly and Moth Magic

Steve Andrews

Winchester, UK
Washington, USA

JOHN HUNT PUBLISHING

First published by Moon Books, 2023
Moon Books is an imprint of John Hunt Publishing Ltd., No. 3 East Street, Alresford
Hampshire SO24 9EE, UK
office@jhpbooks.net
www.johnhuntpublishing.com
www.moon-books.net

For distributor details and how to order please visit the 'Ordering' section on our website.

ISBN: 978 1 80341 052 4
978 1 80341 053 1 (ebook)
Library of Congress Control Number: 2021949062

A CIP catalogue record for this book is available from the British Library.

Design: Matthew Greenfield

UK: Printed and bound by CPI Group (UK) Ltd, Croydon, CR0 4YY
Printed in North America by CPI GPS partners

Contents

Introduction 1
Butterflies 3
Did the Brimstone inspire the word "Butterfly?"
The Monarch is also known as "The Wanderer" 4
The Large Blue's caterpillars need the help of ants 10
The Painted Lady is an amazing migrant 12
Why the Swallowtail is so rare 14
The Comma has its own punctuation mark 16
The Peacock's beauty is its defence 18
Butterflies live in cold places too 19
Hibernating butterflies 23

Moths 26
Why the Death's Head Hawk-moth became a film-star
The Cinnabar's warning colours 28
How the female Emperor Moth can attract a male from a mile away 30
The Mother Shipton was named after a witch and prophetess 31
Wingless Moths 33
The Peppered Moth has a stick caterpillar 37
Moth caterpillars that live in wood 40
Moths that disguise themselves as bees and wasps 42
The Buff-tip Moth looks like a broken twig 45
Not a hummingbird but a hawk-moth 46
The Lobster Moth and Puss Moth 48

Butterfly Gardening 52
After Dark 59
And finally 62

Introduction

British Butterflies and their transformations: arranged and illustrated in a series of plates by H.N. Humphreys, with characters and descriptions by J.O. Westwood (1940)

Who can fail to be amazed by the transformation of a tiny egg into a caterpillar, then into a chrysalis, and finally emerging as a beautiful butterfly? This seemingly magical process is the life cycle of every butterfly and moth. I know that this was one of the many wonders of nature that fascinated me when I was a little boy, and still does so today. To watch this transformation take place is a joy to behold. Keeping caterpillars as a child was part of my introduction to the world of nature, and it was to be part of a strong connection with the natural world that has stayed with me ever since. So many times I have wondered what some crawling caterpillar, perhaps arrayed in colourful spots and stripes, or maybe covered in fur, would one day become? The life cycle of these insects is a key to the magic of nature.

Butterflies and moths have incredible behaviour that we can wonder at too. Many species embark on very long migrations that cross land and sea. How do these fragile-looking little creatures manage to do this? Some species have the most amazing camouflage and others employ other means of protection, including rendering themselves poisonous by eating a toxic diet as larvae. Some moths disguise themselves as insects that can sting, in the hope that would-be predators will leave them well alone.

Butterflies and moths have always fascinated and inspired us and some species have had superstitions evolve around them. The lives of these creatures are as mysterious as they are beautiful. Lepidopterists are continuing to learn more about them each day. There are butterflies and moths that can be found in most parts of the planet, even in the Arctic Circle. Like us, they have colonised nearly all regions of the globe, although sadly today, many species are declining fast mostly due to the threat of pesticides, habitat destruction, and climate change. I would like to think that by understanding more about these incredible insects that more can be done to save them. Hopefully this book will play a part in raising awareness about butterflies and moths, and the magic of these winged wonders of nature.

Butterflies

Did the Brimstone inspire the word "butterfly"?

We all know what a butterfly looks like but have you ever wondered about the origin of the name? There is a species that has been thought to be the insect that inspired the term. The male Brimstone Butterfly (*Gonepteryx rhamni*) has bright sulphur-yellow wings. Could this British and European butterfly be the insect the word butterfly was created to describe?

The Brimstone is a widely distributed butterfly found in the UK, across Europe, in North Africa, also in Turkey, and extending its range as far as Mongolia and Western Siberia. It is a species that hibernates and males can often be seen flying on the warmer days of early spring when there are very few other butterflies about, if any. They can be easily distinguished from the females that are a cream colour with a faint tinge of greenish on the underwings.

The Brimstone caterpillar can only feed on species of Buckthorn, and in the UK, this means the Buckthorn (*Rhamnus cathartica*) or the Alder Buckthorn (*Frangula alnus*). Both types of buckthorns are shrubs that can grow into small trees. They both have berries, and the second species is sometimes known as the Berry-bearing Alder. The Buckthorn is found in woodland and hedges on calcareous soils, whereas the Alder Buckthorn has a liking for acidic soils, so has a tendency to grow where there is a lot of peat, in bogland, on heaths and woodland in these areas. Like most butterflies, the Brimstone is found where the foodplants of its caterpillars grow. Neither species of buckthorn that grows in the UK is particularly common, although they are widely distributed. This means that you will only expect to see Brimstones flying if either type of buckthorn is found in the area. With this in mind, and as a splendid example of butterfly conservation in action, in 2019, the city of Hull had some 3,000 buckthorns planted and gained itself the title of "Butterfly City."

There are some other yellow butterflies seen in Europe, with the Clouded Yellow (*Colias crocea*) being the most commonly seen, but it is the Brimstone that has been considered the most likely contender for being the insect the word butterfly was coined to describe.

The Monarch is also known as "The Wanderer"

The Monarch Butterfly (*Danaus plexippus*) is probably the most well-known butterfly in the world, having been made famous by its incredible yearly migrations across North America, but it is also known as "The Wanderer" and "Milkweed Butterfly." All its names are very descriptive. With its large reddish-orange wings that are veined with black, it is surely regal in its appearance, its caterpillars only feed on species of milkweed (*Asclepias* spp.), and besides being a migratory insect, it has a tendency to wander and colonise new areas if it finds its food-plants growing there. The Monarch was not native to the Canary Islands, or mainland Spain and Portugal, but has successfully established colonies in all these places after the Tropical Milkweed (*A. curassavica*) became a widely cultivated garden flower, and also the Balloon Plant (*Gomphocarpus fruticosus*), which is closely related to the milkweeds, became naturalised in some regions. It is thought that the Monarch first colonised the Canary Islands in 1860 but I don't think anyone knows for certain. As a matter of interest though, the Monarchs found in these European countries are non-migratory butterflies, unlike their cousins in America. This is because they are able to breed all year round and complete their life-cycles because the temperatures never get cold enough to kill the milkweeds, and it is warm enough for the butterflies to be flying, at least in coastal regions. In Canada and North America this is not the case because the winter brings months of sub-zero temperatures and snow and ice. Here the Monarchs long ago evolved, not to hibernate, but to migrate thousands of miles from the cold northern states down to the warmer parts of Florida, California and Mexico. Here they stay semi-dormant roosting on pine trees over the winter months until spring when they fly north as the weather warms. The females lay eggs on milkweed they find along the route northwards but do not complete the trip as far as the most northerly states and Canada. Caterpillars hatch and grow, eventually pupating and then emerging as new Monarchs, and it is these butterflies that take to the wing to continue the migration back to the northern parts they live in.

In places like the Canary Islands and southern Portugal and Spain, there is no need for migration and the Monarchs there are non-migratory ones. However, this means they live as adult butterflies for a much shorter time than the American overwintering Monarch butterflies, which live from late fall until spring. Resident Monarchs only have a couple of weeks as adults and then the cycle begins again. There are also Monarchs in Australia and New Zealand, and here there are populations that have become migratory too due to colder winter months.

The Monarch evolves and adapts to new territories it colonises but can only reproduce if there are milkweeds present. This butterfly is a very rare migrant to the UK but is unable to establish itself there because there are no milkweed species growing wild or in gardens. It will be interesting to see what happens as Climate Change progresses, if the insect moves further north in Europe, and if it will evolve new migratory behaviour. One thing is for certain, the caterpillars will only eat species in the Asclepias and Gomphocarpus genera. These plants are important to them because they contain toxins that the larvae absorb into their bodies and this makes them poisonous as adult butterflies. This is why both caterpillars and adults wear warning colours of bold patterning. The larvae have yellow, white and black stripes, and the butterflies have prominent black veins across their reddish-orange wings. These colours tell would-be predators not to eat them. In North America there is a butterfly that takes all this one step further. The Viceroy (*Limenitis archippus*) mimics the Monarch to fool birds and other creatures that might attack it. This is an example of Mullerian mimicry, in which two or more species have evolved a similar appearance to act as a defence against predators. The Viceroy was long thought to be non-toxic but experiments have shown it to be distasteful for birds too. I think that mimicry in nature is another form of magic in the natural world.

Getting back to the Monarch, this butterfly, with its spectacular looks and equally spectacular migration, has attracted a lot of attention. Many people have felt motivated to help the species survive and there are a large number of groups and organisations in America for people who wish to learn what they can do to help the Monarch. The butterfly faces many threats to its survival today. Herbicides and pesticides are commonly used by farmers and gardeners, and these poisons are a serious danger for the Monarch. Habitat destruction is another problem, and so are the weather extremes caused by Climate Change. Many people, who decide to help these butterflies, grow Milkweeds and look after the caterpillars and chrysalises. Some people are involved in tagging this butterfly so that it can be identified amongst migrant butterflies found a long distance away from where it was originally tagged. Members of Monarch groups exchange tips on looking after these butterflies and seek advice. These people also enjoy sharing photos of butterflies they have cared for or spotted in their gardens. It's not all joy though for people who enjoy helping these butterflies because sometimes tragedy strikes in various ways. Sometimes a caring caterpillar keeper will run out of food for the hungry butterfly larvae, and in desperation buy Milkweed plants from a gardening centre or nursery, only to see the poor creatures dying the next day. This is because plants that are on sale have often been treated with insecticides. This is why growing your own plants is best.

Another problem is a disease caused by a protozoan parasite commonly known as OE. This stands for *Ophryocystis elektroscirrha,* which is a bit of a mouthful. It spreads by tiny spores eaten by caterpillars and it causes varying degrees of weakness in emerging butterflies, as well as deformities. Many Monarchs infected with this are unable to expand their developing wings properly and end up unable to fly, as cripples with deformed wings. Others fail to emerge and get stuck in the chrysalis casing. Monarch carers are well aware of OE and may run tests to see if butterflies are infected. Many people who look after Monarch caterpillars rinse Milkweed used as food in very diluted bleach and water. The cleaning agent is known to kill OE spores.

Another serious problem can be caused by the parasitic tachinid fly. This insect's parasitic larva lives inside the Monarch caterpillar, gradually eating away at its living host. The caterpillar fails to form a normal chrysalis and instead a tachinid fly pupa is formed. It can be really disappointing when this happens but is all part of the natural world and the food-chain of life. Personally, I regard myself as lucky because I got to learn about parasitic flies and wasps when I was a boy, a boy who liked to keep caterpillars to find out what butterfly or moth they would turn into eventually. Sometimes I was rewarded with a spindly looking ichneumon wasp or an ugly fly or flies. Parasites have incredible life cycles too and I learned to appreciate them for this, though it is much easier to delight in a pretty butterfly or attractive moth. Who is to say what is beautiful or ugly and why should one creature have any more right to life than another? It is all part of the magic and mystery of life. People who feel drawn to doing what they can to help Monarchs soon begin to learn about other faces of the natural world. They also are taking action as conservationists. The world needs people doing their part in helping Mother Earth, and caring for Monarch butterflies is a great way for people to start taking personal action.

Monarch butterflies can be very inspiring, not only because

of their great physical beauty but because of their determination to live and reproduce their kind. I will never forget a female Monarch that came my way when I lived in Tenerife. I used to rent an apartment with a balcony outside, and here I grew Milkweed and other plants. I had a pet cat called Tiggy and one day she caught a female Monarch that had come into the balcony. I rushed to try and save the insect and was at first horrified, thinking I was too late. The butterfly was no longer moving and had lost a rear wing. I put it up on a wall that was too high for my cat to get on. The next thing I knew was that the butterfly had made a miraculous recovery and had flown away, even though it was one wing short. I kept some pots with Tropical Milkweed growing in them on the top of this wall, and amazingly within an hour's time the same female Monarch had returned and was laying eggs on the potted plants. I could see it was her because she only had three wings. Even more amazingly she continued doing this for the next 10 days or so, and I ended up with lots of caterpillars, all of which were her sons and daughters. She showed that she had a memory of a place where the plant she needed grew, she showed that she wasn't afraid even though she nearly lost her life there, and she continued with her role in life as a butterfly mother by laying her eggs on the right food-plant, and doing all this even though she only had three wings.

The Monarch has also inspired me to write a song entitled Butterfly In My Beard, and it has proved to be very popular with audiences. I tell them it is based around some real incidents in my life because I really have had a Monarch Butterfly on my beard and I have been called a "Bugman " in the news. This latter reference is to when I was once in the South Wales Echo in an article with the title "CATCH THE BUG - Special World of Insects For Steve." It goes on to describe how "Bugman Steve Andrews likes to come close to the world of insects," and features a colour photo of me with a Madagascan Hissing Cockroach on my forehead and a giant Australian stick insect on my hand. The song lyrics include: "They called me a Bugman on the news one time, they called me a Bugman on the news one time, they called me a Bugman on the news, a Hissing Cockroach on my head got plenty of views, they called me a Bugman on the news one time." In the next verse I sing "make a butterfly and fly with me, say, yeah." I show everyone how to make butterflies with their open palms like wings linked by crossed thumbs to symbolise antennae. This encourages audience participation and makes the song a memorable one. For added effect I place a brooch that looks like a Monarch in my beard. I have a recording of the song included on my album Songs of the Now and Then, which was produced by Jayce Lewis and was released on Bandcamp. There is a video to go with it too in which an animated Monarch follows me about and finally lands, predictably, on my beard.

Butterfly In My Beard
I had a butterfly in my beard, say, yeah,
I had a butterfly in my beard, say yeah,
I had a butterfly in my beard,
It looked pretty strange, it looked pretty weird,
I had a butterfly in my beard, say, yeah.
They called me a Bugman in the news, one time,
They called me a Bugman in the news, one time,
They called me a Bugman in the news,
A Hissing Cockroach on my head got plenty of views,
They called me a Bugman on the news, one time.
Make a butterfly and fly with me, say, yeah,
Make a butterfly and fly with me, say, yeah,
Make a butterfly and fly with me,
Go anywhere and be really free,
Make a butterfly and fly with me, say, yeah.

On another memorable occasion I was commissioned to write a feature about Monarch Butterflies of The Tenerife Sun newspaper, which I had a regular column in at the time. The caption for my article announced "Nine green bottles of butterfly magic potion." It was making reference to the delicate mint-green colouration of the chrysalises of this butterfly, and these chrysalises also have a row of exquisite minute golden dots around them. This pupal stage of the butterfly is the time when the magic of transformation takes place, when all that was a crawling and eating caterpillar is broken down and rearranged in the mould that will turn out a butterfly. Of course, this happens with all species of butterflies and moths. The chrysalises, pupae, and cocoons for moths, are like little magic boxes. They are also often incredibly beautiful in themselves, like tiny artistic sculptures.

The Large Blue's caterpillars need the help of ants

Large Blue and Chalkhill Blue vars. Richard South (1906)

The Large Blue (*Phengaris arion*), as its name suggests is, for a blue butterfly, very large with a wingspan of up to two inches. Aptly named, this butterfly has blue wings that are marked with rows of black dots on the forewings. The insect is a really interesting species of British butterfly on two counts. Firstly, it is a wonderful example of how a species can be brought back from extinction after it has become extinct in one place, just as long as it hasn't died out everywhere. The Large Blue was successfully reintroduced to the UK in a very carefully executed conservation plan that used livestock from Sweden. At time of writing there are 11 colonies of Large Blues surviving at secret locations in England.

Secondly, because it is a butterfly that has a parasitic relationship with species of ants, and, in fact, depends on these insects to be able to complete its life-cycle. Yes, you read that correctly: ants! The Large Blue butterfly's caterpillar is a parasite of the red ant species (*Myrmica subuleti*). In early stages of the caterpillar's life it feeds on the flowering parts of Wild Thyme (*Thymus polytrichus*) and Marjoram (*Origanum vulgare*) but then in the last instar (stage), it drops to the ground and stops feeding on plants. It is hoping to be discovered by a worker ant. The butterfly caterpillar successfully mimics an ant larva by secreting pheromones that the ant mistakes for those of its own species. It also feeds the worker ant that has found it with a drop of a secretion the ant enjoys. Sometime after this, the deceived ant then carries the caterpillar back to the ant nest, where the caterpillar will betray its host by feeding on the ant larvae and pupae. It must successfully maintain this deception, and it has been found that the first 10 days after arrival in the ant nest are the most critical. Failure to fool the ants will mean the Large Blue caterpillar's death. The caterpillar lives in the ant nest throughout the winter before pupating the following year. As a chrysalis it is tended and kept clean by worker ants. Eventually when it emerges from the pupa in May, June or July, depending on location, it makes its way out of the nest and dries its wings out after climbing on to some vegetation.

The Large Blue was never common in the UK but became extinct in 1979. This butterfly's numbers have been drastically declining in its continental range too, and it is considered an endangered species globally. Besides needing the right type of ant species to parasitise, this butterfly needs the right sort of habitat for its host to be found in, as well as somewhere its food plants grow. It is not surprising it has become so very rare when you consider how specialised this butterfly's needs are. Actually this is the case with very many species. They require the correct habitats and availability of the right types of plants, and in the blue butterflies, this extends to the right types of ants. There are many other species of blue that have larvae that are tended by ant species. It is all part of the amazing complexity of the natural world.

The Painted Lady is an amazing migrant

The Painted Lady (*Vanessa cardui*) is an incredible butterfly for a number of reasons, and not just because, as its name suggests, it is a very pretty insect. It has perhaps colonised more of the planet than any other species and it takes part in amazingly long migrations that easily compare with those of the Monarch. Its distribution is listed as cosmopolitan, with the exception of South America. The Painted Lady is a permanent resident of Africa where it can be found all year round, but it migrates northwards over Europe as far as the Arctic Circle. It has even been reported occasionally from Iceland. It also lives in the Canary Islands and Madeira but migrations take place in spring that take the butterfly all over Europe and into the UK.

The Painted Lady, unlike most butterflies, has a very wide range of plants that its caterpillars can feed upon. There are species in the Cucurbitaceae, Asteraceae, Fabaceae, Brassicaceae, Vitaceae, Malvaceae and Boraginaceae. Food plants include many species of Thistle, Stinging Nettle (*Urtica dioica*), Mallows (*Malva spp.*), and Viper's Bugloss (*Echium spp.*). There are over 300 plant species in total that this butterfly's caterpillars have been found on.

Every butterfly is a winged wonder, an amazing living creature but the Painted Lady is extra special because of its migratory behaviour, which for a long time was a mystery. Scientists didn't know whether these butterflies left the UK and northern countries of Europe in the autumn and headed south again or if they died as the winter took hold but were seen again the following year because of new arrivals that had migrated. A team of research scientists from the University of York, in partnership with researchers from other organisations, including Butterfly Conservation and NERC (Centre for Ecology & Hydrology and Rothamsted Research), finally solved the mystery. The results of studies were published in *Ecography*, and revealed that the Painted Lady butterfly makes an incredible 9,000 mile round trip on its migratory journey. Butterflies from the UK do leave the country in the autumn when it is getting colder. They migrate south at very high altitudes, which is why they have not been seen before. The insects fly and are carried by air currents as high as 500 metres above the ground. In favourable conditions they can reach an amazing 30mph. The Painted Lady 's migration is double that of the Monarch. The Painted Lady migrates from Tropical Africa northward to the shores of the UK and to other countries of northern Europe and into the Arctic Circle, and then travels back southwards when the cold sets in. Like the Monarch, there are more than one generation needed to complete the migration, and as many as six generations of butterflies can take part. Unlike the migratory Monarchs that stop off for the winter in warmer States of America, the Painted Lady just keeps on going. Richard Fox, Surveys Manager for Butterfly Conservation, who was involved in the studies, described this butterfly's annual journey as "astonishing."

Why The Swallowtail is so rare

Swallowtail Butterfly. Male and female with caterpillars and chrysalids. Richard South (1906)

The Swallowtail Butterfly (*Papilio machaon britannicus*) is the largest butterfly native to Britain, and it is also one of the rarest species. It can only be seen flying in some parts of the Norfolk Broads. The European variety (*P. machaon gorganus*) is a far more commonly seen and widely distributed insect found in many parts of southern Europe. There are other subspecies as well. It appears that the cause of the rarity of the British Swallowtail is due to the chosen food-plant not being a common species either. In the UK the caterpillar of the Swallowtail feeds on Milk Parsley (*Peucedanum palustre*), a plant which grows in wetland areas. The European Swallowtail's caterpillar can eat a far wider range of plants, including Wild Carrot (*Daucus carota*), Fennel (*Foeniculum vulgare*) and Rue (*Ruta graveolens*). This gives the butterfly a far greater range of habitats. Not only that but the British Swallowtail only produces one brood each year, whereas the continental subspecies produces several.

I was delighted to discover Swallowtails in the garden of the house I have been living in Portugal. The females lay their eggs on Rue, a commonly grown garden plant here. Imagine my surprise to see a butterfly which is a great rarity in Britain flitting around in the front garden of the place I was renting. I was soon to discover Swallowtails in urban and rural settings. The reason being, as I have explained, that the European subspecies is nowhere near as fussy as its British counterpart because the larva of the Swallowtail found in Europe, will accept a wide range of food-plants. Having said that, in my experience, the caterpillars will only eat the plants they have already been feeding on.

Where I live this is always Rue, though I am well aware that many people find them feeding on Fennel in other parts of Portugal. In the area I am in the Fennel normally dies back early and the summers are too hot and dry for it to have any foliage. The Rue is an evergreen and is generally kept watered in gardens so provides a food source all year round. It seems that the local population of Swallowtails have adapted to local conditions by choosing Rue as the plant on which the females deposit their eggs. To my mind it is like seeing an example of the Darwinian Theory of Evolution in action. The butterfly appears to be adapting to its circumstances. Presumably if conditions remained like this after generations yet another subspecies could evolve that would only use Rue as a larval food-plant, in the same way that the British Swallowtail will only use Milk Parsley.

Otherwise, besides the choice of plants the caterpillars will eat, the two butterflies are very similar. They are both attractively patterned in bold yellow and black and with projections to the hindwings, hence the name. There are also blue and red markings at the edges of the hindwings. The British variety is slightly smaller and the black is blacker but you really need to be a butterfly specialist to tell them apart when it comes to what they look like. The caterpillars look much the same. They are a bright shade of lime green, striped with black and dotted with orange. If disturbed, they protrude a forked orange-coloured organ from the top of the head area. This is an osmeterium, It emits an unpleasant smell and is a means of defence. Of course, the bold colouration of adult butterflies and caterpillars are warning colours, signifying that this species has an unpleasant taste and is toxic to varying degrees. The Swallowtail caterpillar bears a passing resemblance to the larvae of the Monarch too. The chrysalises of the subspecies *gorganus* come in two forms. A light green one is for the spring, summer and autumn broods and a brown one is for the last generation, and this chrysalis is how this species passes the winter. It can be seen flying in every month apart from January. It is such a beautiful butterfly with such striking colours that seeing it is always a real delight whatever time of year it may be.

The Comma has its own punctuation mark

Comma Butterfly Artist: Jacob Hubner (1761-1826)

The Comma Butterfly (*Polygonia c-album*) takes its name from a white marking on the underside of its hindwings, a marking that bears a strong resemblance to a comma punctuation mark. Otherwise the undersides of its wings are mottled in shades of brown and look just like dead leaves. They have frayed edges too and this completes the camouflage. The upper side of the Comma's wings are a tawny-orange marked with black dots. It is an attractive butterfly with an unusual shape to the wings due to the raggedness which makes the wings look like leaves when folded and viewed from the side. The caterpillar of the Comma also relies on camouflage as a form of protection. It has a combination of grayish-brown and a large white marking over much of its body and this makes the creature resemble the droppings of a bird. The caterpillars live singly and will feed on a wide range of plants. Hop (*Humulus lupulus*), Stinging Nettle (*Urtica dioica*), Gooseberry (*Ribes*), Currant (*Ribes spp.*), Elm (*Ulmus spp.*) and Willow (*Salix spp.*) are amongst the species it has been found on.

The Comma is a species of butterfly that is actually increasing its range and numbers, while many other species are declining in numbers. It wasn't always this way, though, and from the mid-1800s the insect had been suffering a decline. It is thought that this was because Hops were being used as its main food-plant and this crop became grown a lot less. These days the caterpillar of the Comma is most often found on Stinging Nettles. It is one of the five British butterflies that use this plant. The others are the Small Tortoiseshell (*Aglais urticae*), the Peacock (*A. io*), the Red Admiral (*Vanessa atalanta*) and the Painted Lady (*V. cardui*). All five are members of the Nymphalidae family of butterflies. They are all good examples of why a plant that is thought of as a weed can be very important as the food of a species of insect. I remember having an argument on the BBC Community forums about this. He had admitted he used Roundup (Glyphosate) herbicide on his farm but maintained it was no danger to wildlife. I said that I had seen this used to destroy patches of Stinging Nettles, and I pointed out that this plant feeds the caterpillars of five species of butterflies. "How can you kill this plant without harming them?", I asked. He had no answer.

The Comma hibernates and its dead-leaf appearance helps disguise it then. This means it can be found all year round, flying late into the autumn and waking up on warm days in winter too. It can be seen on the blossoms of the Ivy late in the year. After it wakes in spring the butterflies can give rise to a summer generation, which are known as the *hutchinsoni* form. They are much lighter in colouration. Butterflies that this summer brood are the parents of have the normal darker colours to their wings, colours which help their winter camouflage. While it is easy to understand how the Comma's resemblance to a dead leaf helps hide it from predators, the white marking like a punctuation mark remains a mystery.

The Peacock's beauty is its defence

The Peacock Butterfly (*Aglais io*), for many people, is the most beautiful of all species of British butterflies. With its four eye-spots, with one on each wing, it is unmistakable. The background colour of its wings is a rich rusty-red and the eyespots are black, blue and yellow. By sharp contrast the undersides of the wings are very drab. They are coloured a very dark brown, almost black. When the wings are closed it is very difficult to see the insect if it is resting on a tree trunk or other dark natural background. It blends in so well it disappears. The edges of the wings are also ragged looking and this combination of colouration and form, like in the case of the Comma, produce an insect that looks more like a dead leaf than anything alive. Like the Comma, too, the Peacock uses this camouflage as part of its defence tactics when hibernating through the winter months. The Peacock is almost like two butterflies in one. There is the dark one that can easily hide away going unnoticed and there is also the brightly coloured one that flies in the sunshine and is very hard to miss. This latter face of the Peacock is used to scare would-be predators, however, because the eyespots make it look like the face of a larger animal. If the wings are flashed open suddenly this will startle and confuse a possible enemy too. In addition to this, the Peacock Butterfly is able to make a hissing sound with its wings. This is used to scare off mice and rats that may attack the butterflies when they are hiding away in dark places for the winter. In the dark, the colourful display of the wings has no effect but a hissing sound, like a snake, does the trick.

Peacocks emerge from hibernation in March or April. The male butterflies only mate once and do not live as long as the females. The males are territorial and will perch on a high spot to survey anything flying into their space. If it is a rival male it will be chased away and if it is an unmated female, it will be pursued as a potential mate.

Female Peacocks usually lay their eggs on Stinging Nettles but Hops and the Small Nettle (*U. urens*) are other reported food-plants. The caterpillars are blackish in colour and live in a communal web. There is usually only one generation in a year and butterflies hatch late in July. In late summer they can often be seen on the Buddleia or Butterfly Bush, in autumn they will take rotting fruit and can be seen on many late flowering garden flowers. The Peacock is a frequent visitor to gardens and parks but is equally at home in countryside locations, such as clearings in woodlands and along riverbanks. Besides the UK, the Peacock is also found in many parts of Europe, in Asia and right over as far as Japan. Wherever it flies it is without any doubt one of the most beautiful butterflies in the world.

Butterflies live in cold places too

We all tend to think of butterflies as colourful winged creatures that live in warm, sunny places, so it may well come as a surprise to readers to discover there are species that live in the Arctic and far north. In the UK, the Scotch Argus (*Erebia aethiops*) is a butterfly found in northern and western parts of southern

Scotland in the UK, and in Palaearctic regions of Europe, the Alps, the Balkans, Asia Minor, the Urals, and Caucasus. Also in Britain, there are two known colonies in Cumbria in northern England. It is a member of the Satyrinae family and very similar to many of the other butterflies in the Ringlets group. The Scotch Argus has dark brown to blackish-brown wings with reddish-yellow bands that contain three black eye-spots with white pupils. Other types of Ringlet have different numbers of these eye-spots and differences in wing colouration. The Scotch Argus flies from June to August and its caterpillars, like so many species in the Satyrinae family of "Browns," feed on grass species. Purple Moor-grass (*Molinia caerulea*) and Blue Moor-grass (*Sesleria caerulea*) are two of this butterfly's favourite food-plants, and the names of these grasses give a clue to the kind of location this species frequents. It can be found on moors, hillsides and grassy locations. The Arran Brown (*E. ligea*) is very similar and sounds like it is a British species from the Isle of Arran. However, this is debatable, and is due to the fact that specimens exist in historical collections of the Scotch Argus that date back to 1803, when it was recorded as from this island in the Clyde Isles. Perhaps it once lived in Scotland but has since become extinct?

Today there is uncertainty about this species The Arran Brown is known to live in south-eastern and northern Europe, including parts of Scandinavia, including Finland. It flies in July and August in open woodland, at forest edges, in clearings and other grassy places. Its caterpillars feed on a variety of grasses and sedges and take two years to become ready to transform into a chrysalis and then to emerge as butterflies. The Arran Brown can be mistaken for the Arctic Ringlet (*E. disa*) and the Lapland Ringlet (*E. embla*) but can be distinguished by white blotches on the underside of its hindwings. The Arctic Ringlet, as its name suggests, is found in Arctic areas, including Arctic Europe, Arctic Russia and Arctic North America. It prefers subarctic damp woodlands and Arctic bogs. The Lapland Ringlet is found in Scandinavia, Russia, Siberia and as far as North Korea. Making everything even more complex, and why you really need to be a Ringlet expert to be sure about identification, this species has three subspecies. It is found in sunny parts and clearings in spruce and pine forests, in marshes and on moors. Yet another Ringlet found in the far north is the Arctic Woodland Ringlet (*E. polaris*). It lives in Arctic Norway and Finland, as well as in the Urals and North Siberia, where it flies in June and July in river valleys, open woodland and meadows.

These species of Ringlet butterflies are not the only butterflies that can be found in cold Arctic lands. The Pale Arctic Clouded Yellow (*Colias nastes*) is one more such butterfly that braves the inhospitable reaches of the far north but it is a member of the Pieridae, the family which includes the far more common Large (*Pieris brassicae*) and Small White (*Artogeia rapae*) butterflies. In fact, the pale Arctic Clouded Yellow inhabits northerly parts of Norway, Sweden and Finland, where in the locations it does live in, it can sometimes be found in hundreds. It flies from mid-May to August, depending on location, and lives on marshy areas, rocky and grassy slopes, scrubland and heathland. This butterfly has even been reported from Greenland. The Pale Arctic Clouded Yellow is a strong-flier. The males have delicate greenish-white or yellowish-white with grey to blackish borders to the wings, and the females have more dark markings and a greyish dusting to the yellowish wings. The caterpillars are reported to feed on various legumes, including Alpine Milkvetch (*Astragalus alpinus*) and blueberry (*Vaccinium* spp.) This Arctic-living butterfly is also known as the Labrador Sulphur and can be found in Alaska, Canada, the Rocky Mountains, Washington, as well as parts of Russia, Siberia, China and Mongolia. It has many subspecies, which isn't surprising considering the large range it has colonised and how it has survived in often bleak and inhospitable conditions.

Besides the Ringlets and a Clouded Yellow, there are several species of Fritillary butterfly that live in Arctic regions. The fritillaries are all in the Nymphalidae, a large family that includes some other butterflies in this book. The Polar Fritillary (*Clossiana polaris*) is well-named. This species has the typical mainly orange wings chequered with darker markings. It is circumpolar in its range, though very local and uncommon wherever it is found. It flies over open tundra from May to August and the caterpillars feed on species of blueberry and Mountain Avens (*Dryas octopetala*). Closely related is another fritillary with a suitably cold and northern name, Thor's Fritillary (*C. thore*), named after the hammer-wielding god of Norse mythology, this butterfly is found in the Alps, Norway, Sweden and Northern Finland. It lives in wooded clearings, shaded areas of forests and in wood margins. The caterpillars feed on various Violet (*Viola* spp.), a food-plant for many fritillaries found in warmer parts of the world. The caterpillar may need two years to complete its life as a larva.

From Thor's Fritillary we next take a look at Freya's Fritillary (*C. freija*), yet another fritillary species named after a character from Old Norse and Viking mythology. Freya was, of course, the goddess of love, fertility, battles and death. This particular species of fritillary is found in much of Scandinavia and also in Balkan areas. This butterfly has been found on grassy slopes of Norway, Sweden and Finland, where its larvae feed on various plants, including blueberry/bilberry species.

Finally, in the fritillary species, we are taking a look at those that are found in some of the colder parts of the planet, and we next discover the Lapland Fritillary (*Hypodryas iduna*). This butterfly is truly a Polar and Subpolar species with its range covering Northern Fennoscandia, and over to Siberia. It can be found flying from the Arctic Circle all the way to the Arctic Sea. It prefers heathland and marshy areas and bogs, and is on the wing in June and July. The male has the usual orange background colour, chequered with darker markings and lines but also has a lot of grey colouration. They fly close to the ground to shelter from the winds and also are known to seek shelter among the Dwarf Birch (*Betula nana*) trees. The caterpillars of the Lapland Fritillary feed on Alpine Speedwell (*Veronica alpina*), Plantain (*Plantago*) and Vaccinium species. They are gregarious larvae and feed and hibernate in groups

It may well come as a surprise to learn that this is only a fraction of the butterflies that can be found in the Arctic, and is a perfect example of how life can adapt and find a way in the most unlikely places. The wildfires being caused and exacerbated by the Climate Crisis cannot be helping though, especially those species that already have a limited range and a long life-cycle in difficult conditions.

Hibernating Butterflies

After taking a look at the butterfly species that live their lives in very cold locations, let us now find out about some of those that hibernate through the winter months. In the UK, there are several well-known species that find somewhere safe to sleep until the spring. You may have come across a butterfly in your house and wondered why it was there and what to do about it. The most commonly found species that comes indoors is the Small Tortoiseshell (*Aglais urticae*). This is a very pretty species that was one of the most frequently seen butterflies in the UK, though over the past several years its numbers have been declining. It is nevertheless still widely distributed and there's no shortage of its food-plant, which is the Stinging Nettle.

The Small Tortoiseshell looks for a secluded and dry place to hide away for the winter, and if it is in a hole in a tree, in a barn, shed, or outhouse, it may have chosen wisely and be able to stay dormant until the spring arrives. However, if the butterfly has come into a house via an open door or window, it may end up in trouble. For example, if it has chosen an unheated and unused room, it might be lucky and be undisturbed, but if the homeowner decides to use the room and puts the heating on then the butterfly will wake up and want to go back outside. If it is seen and let out in spring there's no problem but what happens if it is in the depths of winter and still far too cold outside?

Butterflies in situations like this need carefully moving to somewhere they can complete their hibernation in peace. They need somewhere that stays cool and dry, and that has a way they can get out when the world warms up. Ideally you can move the butterfly to a new location to continue its period of dormancy but if this is not possible the next best option is to release the insect on a mild and sunny day, on which it could stand a chance of finding new hibernating quarters. I remember an incident a few years back when I was recording at Jayce Lewis's Northstone Studios near Bridgend. It was late autumn and a Small Tortoiseshell had decided that Jayce's drum-room was where it would sleep away the winter months. I ended up taking it out and putting the butterfly on some thick ivy that was growing up a tree near the studios. It was a sunny day so the insect had a chance to find somewhere else to go for its winter sleep. The Peacock is another species of butterfly that may come into a house or building for the winter, and the same situation and means of solving it apply.

Three more British butterflies that hibernate are the Comma, the Brimstone and the Red Admiral. The Comma usually hibernates in woodland, choosing hollow trees and woodpiles, but also in gardens in sheds and outhouses. It flies late in the autumn, though, and can be seen with Red Admirals on Ivy blossom and on rotting fruit. The Brimstone hibernates in wooded areas too and is capable of sleeping in freezing conditions holding on tight to a twig or other surface. This butterfly has a very long life-span for a butterfly and can live 10 months or even a year. It will hibernate for seven months of this, from September to April. The male Brimstones awake before the females, though, and can be spotted on mild days in February and in March. The females sleep a bit longer because the buckthorn bushes need to be in bud for them to lay their eggs after mating. If they awake too early in spring the branches will be bare. Finally, the Red Admiral (*Vanessa atalanta*) is the last of the British butterflies that gets through the winter in adult form. There is, however, a lot of doubt and debate about whether this species really does hibernate like the other butterflies, and whether it seeks out overwintering quarters where it can become dormant. Many authorities think that the Red Admiral merely rests when it is too cold or wet and resumes flying when better weather comes its way. Because of this, the Red Admiral can be seen on very mild days in winter, and I have personally seen them as late as December. Ivy blossoms in flower in the winter sunshine is the place to look. There are usually other pollinators there too, such as Drone Flies, that mimic bees so well. Spotting a Red Admiral in winter is one of those magical moments of life, and its bold red, black and white wings seem to fit the season so well.

Moths

Why the Death's Head Hawk-moth became a film-star

Death's-head hawk-moth (1840)

With a wingspan of up to five inches across, the Death's-Head Hawk-moth is the largest moth to be seen in Britain, although it is not a resident species. No stage of its life-cycle can withstand the winters and this species reaches UK shores as a migrant. It is found in parts of Africa, the Canary Islands, the Mediterranean countries and throughout Europe, as well as from the Middle East over as far as India.

Wherever it can be seen it is certainly going to make a lasting impression, not only because of its large size but because of its bizarre appearance with a marking like a skull on its thorax. If this moth is disturbed it can also squeak quite loudly. This squeaking is thought to mimic the sound of a queen bee, which makes a sound to keep the worker bees calm. This is of potential use to the moth because it has the unusual habit of raiding beehives for honey. This is because it only has a short proboscis so cannot feed on nectar from flowers like other hawk-moth species.

The body of this weird moth is striped with yellow like a hornet, and can also be seen as resembling the ribs of a skeleton. Because of its strange appearance and habits the Death's-head Hawk has become thought of as a creature of ill omen and is the subject of a number of superstitions. Its reputation for being a harbinger of doom, and its scary looks were enough to get this moth a place in the world of films. It is featured in *The Silence of Lambs* (1991), and can be seen in publicity for this horror movie. In this film it is the calling card of serial killer Buffalo Bill. The Death's-head Hawk-moth also gets shown on the big screen in *Dracula* (1958), *The Blood Beast Terror* (1967) and in *Un Chien Andalou* (1929).

The moth gets mentioned in the poem "Ode To Melancholy" by John Keats: "Make not your rosary of yew-berries, Nor let the beetle, nor the death-moth be, your mournful Psyche." This poetic mention alludes to Greek mythology. Psyche was the goddess of the soul. Also, The Fates or Moirai were ancient Greek goddesses who presided over the destiny of humans. Atropos was one of The Fates, and the name meant "Unturnable," which was a metaphor for death. Acheron was a river that was thought of as a pathway to Hades, the Underworld. This explains the scientific name for the Death's-head Hawk-moth, where again it is linked with the world of the dead.

Back in the world of the living the Death's-head Hawk-moth does so well, and is so widely distributed, because of the very large range of plants its caterpillars can feed upon. The larvae will feed on assorted species in the *Cannabaceae, Solanaceae, Verbenaceae, Oleaceae, Bignoniaceae,* and *Pedaliaceae.* In keeping with the moth's connection with death and the darker side of life, perhaps it is no surprise to find that the caterpillars can feed on poisonous plants like the Thorn-apple or Devil's Weed (*Datura stramonium*) and other species in the Nightshade family. Thorn-apple was a common choice of food-plant in Tenerife, where the plant grows as a weed and along roadsides. The larvae will also eat Potato plants, Jasmine (*Jasminum spp*), Privet (*Ligustrum ovalifolium*), Butterfly Bush (*Buddleia davidii*), Lantana (*Lantana camara*), and the Tropical Tulip Tree (*Spathodea nilotica*).

The Death's-head Hawk is constantly brooded and is not long in the pupal state in warm regions. It is buried in the soil but is unable to withstand the cold of British and northern winters. The caterpillars are very large and come in three colour variations: green, yellow or brown. They have the characteristic tail-spike that all hawk-moth larvae have, though in this species the spike is drooping. The caterpillar does not move much but if alarmed it can click its mandibles and even bite. It is a suitably formidable looking creature that looks as if it could eventually turn into the equally weird adult moth.

The Cinnabar's warning colours

The Cinnabar (*Tyria jacobaeae*) is a very brightly coloured moth that looks so pretty that many people often think it is a butterfly, and this mistake is aided by the fact that the insect often flies in the sunshine. The Cinnabar's forewings are black with a rosy-pink line and two dots of the same colour, while the hindwings are the same reddish-pink, delicately bordered with black. The body is black as well. The Cinnabar gets its name from the likeness between the colour of the mineral known as Cinnabar and its colour. The caterpillars are brightly coloured too but this time with a background shade of orange-yellow ringed with black. They make no effort to hide and a bunch of them feeding on a Ragwort (*Senecio jacobaea*) plant is nearly impossible to miss. The moths are seen flying in June and July and are swiftly followed by the larvae which can also be seen in July, and in August too. They will eat Groundsel species as well, and are found in gardens, waste ground, allotments, fields and on sand dunes by the sea, anywhere really where they can find Ragwort or Groundsel species.

The colours of the Cinnabar Moth and its caterpillar are warning colours, and just like those employed by the Monarch Butterfly, they are a sign that they are foul-tasting and toxic. In other words, they are telling a would-be predator that eating them could be an unpleasant mistake. This display is an example of a defence strategy known as "Warning colours." The moth and caterpillar are toxic too because they have absorbed poisons from the plants they have fed upon.

The Cinnabar is found throughout the UK and also in parts of Europe, in western and central Asia, and across Siberia as far as China. It was a very common moth in the UK but like so many species has been declining, though is still plentiful. The Cinnabar has also been introduced into New Zealand, Australia and North America where it was intended as a bio-control to help reduce or eliminate Ragwort weeds. As a matter of interest and concern for conservationists, the Ragwort, according to the charity organisation Buglife, is host to over 30 other species in addition to the Cinnabar Moth. Sadly there has been a campaign in the UK to get rid of the plant, which has been classed as a weed that is dangerous to horses, cattle and livestock. It is true that Ragwort contains toxins that can cause serious harm to the liver of an animal that consumes it but normally the animals will avoid grazing on it in a field. It was included in the Injurious Weeds Act of 1959. The problem arose because of modern ways of harvesting hay in which all the vegetation that has been cut in a field is dried and bundled up to be used as animal feed. If Ragwort has been included a horse cannot detect it if it is dried and included in hay that it is being fed. Cases of proven poisoning from the plant are, however, rare. Nevertheless, Ragwort does need removing if it is growing in a field that will be used for harvesting hay to feed to livestock. Otherwise it is a beautiful and important wildflower that always has many pollinating insects feeding on its golden and starry flowers.

How the female Emperor Moth can attract a male from a mile away

Emperor Moth (Saturnia pavonia) released into Public Domain by author, Algirdas.

The Emperor Moth (*Saturnia pavonia*) is one of the largest resident species of moths found in the UK. It is also the only species found in Britain that is a representative of the very large Silkmoth family or *Saturniidae*. It is like a moth version of the Peacock Butterfly because it has four eyespots prominently displayed on its wings. The female Emperor moth is otherwise mostly greyish or blue-grey in colour. The smaller male is more colourful with a brownish tinge to the grey of his forewings and orange colouration for a large part of the hindwings. The male Emperor also has feathered antennae that add to his attractive appearance. It is with these majestic antennae that he tracks down his mate. Males moths are able to detect the scent of females of their species from a long way away. In the case of the Emperor it is said to be over a mile. The female moth stays resting, often near where she has emerged from her cocoon, and emits pheromones which are carried by air currents and are what male Emperor Moths are seeking. The females only fly under cover of darkness but the male moths are on the wing by day and can be seen flying in the spring sunlight over downs, dunes and moorland where the species is found. It is on the wing from late March until early May and the caterpillars can be found over the summer months. They are large and spectacular, a bright lime-green for the main colouration with black rings and many small yellow tubercules. They can be found living and feeding singly. Caterpillars of the Emperor Moth eat a wide range of plants including Heather (*Erica spp*.), Meadowsweet (*Filipendula ulmaria*), Cinquefoil (*Potentilla spp*.) Alder Blackthorn (*Frangula alnus*), Blackberry (*Rubus fruticosus*), Hawthorn (*Crataegus monogyna*) Blackthorn (*Prunus spinosa*), and Sallows and Willows (*Salix* spp.).

The pupae are formed in fibrous cocoons within which they spend the winter months.

The Emperor Moth is like a smaller version of the closely related but much bigger Giant Peacock Moth (*S. pyri*), which is found in many parts of Europe, and once was the inspiration for some artwork by Vincent van Gogh. Although the moths are very big, they are unable to eat so do not live long. They do all their feeding as caterpillars. As adults they live to find mates and start the cycle off again.

Many of the exotic species of silkmoth are some of the biggest and most attractive moths in the world. The Atlas Moth (*Attacus atlas*), which comes from the forests of Asia, has a wingspan that can reach as much as 24 cm across. The wings are reddish brown with a pattern of black, white, pink, and purple markings making it a most attractive creature. Like other members of the Saturniid moth family though, it does not eat and only lives a week or so. The female, like the female Emperor Moth, attracts a male by emitting pheromones. Often, she will remain right by her cocoon and not fly until after she has mated. This is to conserve energy. It is hard for us to understand how such a spectacular living creature, a true winged wonder, only lives to reproduce and die. It is easy to think there is some sort of dark magic at play, but it is just as easy to see these moths as a miracle of life.

The Mother Shipton was named after a witch and prophetess

The Mother Shipton (*Callistege mi*) is a day-flying moth named after a 16th century witch from Yorkshire. The moth has wings of dark and lighter greyish-brown with creamy-coloured markings, and the forewings have outlines that are thought to depict a witch's face, hence the insect's name. In particular, the wings are thought to look like an engraving from the title page of the 1686 book *The Strange and Wonderful History of Mother Shipton*. However, Mother Shipton, the prophetess, is actually a mainly mythical character, based around a woman known as Ursula Southeil, who was born in 1488. There are many stories and myths about her, and even her surname is in question because it has alternative spellings. Mother Shipton could also have been Ursula Southhill, Ursula Soothtell, or Ursula Sontheil.

Amongst the legends about her is that she is said to have foretold the death of Cardinal Wolsey in 1530. Charles Hindley, a 19th century bookseller, created a poem he claimed was written by Shipton. Whether he wrote it or whether it was really by Mother Shipton, it was certainly prophetic. The poem told of "Carriages without horses and air planes", as well as predicting the end of the world in 1881. Some of the folklore that has come about based around Mother Shipton can be traced to real people and/or places. For example, Mother Shipton's Cave, in Knaresborough, North Yorkshire, is said to be where she was born. This cave has a well very close by that is a "petrifying well," meaning that objects left in its water become covered in mineral deposits in a similar way that stalactites form in caves. This natural process has been said to be proof of the magical powers of Mother Shipton the witch. The cave is the oldest tourist attraction to charge an admittance fee and has been in operation since way back in 1630. Visitors to the well leave objects there so they can become encrusted by the waters, possibly to return at a future date to see how the items they left there have been turned to stone. The objects are usually left strung up in falling water. So successful financially is Mother Shipton's Cave and Well that Mother Shipton's Cave Limited is a local company that was created to take advantage of what a great attraction this place is for tourists.

But getting back to Mother Shipton, the insect, it is a species in the *Erebidae* family of moths. The long, thin, and yellowish-coloured caterpillar has a large range of food-plants, including Clovers, (*Trifolium* sp.), Black Medick (*Medicago lupulina*), Common Knotgrass (*Polygonum aviculare*), Lucerne (*Medicago sativa*), Common Heather (*Calluna vulgaris*), Bird's-foot Trefoil (*Lotus corniculatus*), Cock's-foot Grass (*Dactylis glomeratus*) and other species of grasses.

The Mother Shipton is widely distributed but mainly found on moorland, heaths, waste ground, and other grassy open places. If you ever encounter one of these day-flying moths you can see for yourself the markings on the wing that are said to look like the face of a crone.

Wingless Moths

Vapourer Moth. An illustration from British Entomology by John Curtis (1940s)

A wingless moth sounds like a crippled moth, missing one of the main parts of its body, but there are species of moth that have evolved to have only very tiny rudimentary wings that are totally useless for flight. It is only the females that are like this. Often, they are further disadvantaged by not being able to feed too. Their function in life is to be found by a male with which they will mate, and after this to lay their eggs and then die. This seems very sad, very dark, to a human way of thinking, but in the world of nature it has clearly proved to be a successful adaptation that many species have evolved.

One of the most successful species, and I use "successful" here in relation to how widely distributed the species is, has the name Vapourer Moth (*Orgyia antiqua*), though in America it is more commonly known as the Rusty Tussock Moth. It is in the Lymantriidae, or Lymantriinae family, as it is now known. The male moths are an orange-brown shade of colouration with a white dot on each forewing. They fly by day in bright sunlight, as well as occasionally at night. They have feathered antennae and their aim in life is to find the wingless females that look more like a grub than a moth and that spend their lives clinging to the cocoon that they emerged from. In the same way as the Emperor Moth females attract mates by luring them with the scent of pheromones, so too do the female Vapourer Moths use this method to look for male partners.

After a successful mating the female moth lays her eggs on her old cocoon, where they remain right through the winter before hatching the following year. The caterpillar is a very pretty creature with tufts of coloured hair. Its body is mainly grey but it has many red tubercules, and right along the middle of the back are four toothbrush-like tufts of light yellow hair arising from a black stripe. There are many dark hairs on this caterpillar, and two tufts of black hairs on the head with one each side, as well as another two smaller tufts about halfway along the body, again with one on each side. The male caterpillar is a lot smaller than that of the female. I first discovered these colourful larvae when I was a boy and used to visit my grandparents. There were Flowering Currant bushes in their back garden and there were always Vapourer Moth caterpillars on them every summer. They will also feed on a very wide range of trees and shrubs, including Birch (*Betula pendula*), Blackthorn (*Prunus spinosa*), Blackberry (*Rubus spp.*), Hawthorn (*Crataegus spp.*), Rose (*Rosa spp.*), Lime (*Tilia europaea*), Oak (*Quercus spp.*), Hazel (*Corylus avellana*) and Willow (*Salix spp.*). I used to keep the colourful caterpillars and see them transform into pupae in cocoons and eventually into moths. Seeing the strange flightless females was an early lesson for me in the multitude of ways that life exists.

There is also the very similar Scarce Vapourer Moth (*Telochurus recens*). Its name is very apt because this moth is now very scarce indeed and declining in numbers. The Scarce Vapourer used to be known to science as *Orgyia recens* but has been given its own genus, although it does look much like its cousin The Vapourer. The males fly by day and look much the same, although the main colouring is a deeper brownish-orange and the white marks are near the wingtips and different.

The moth can be found from June to July and the flightless females again lay their eggs on their old cocoons after mating with a male that has found them. The caterpillars, which overwinter as small larvae, are very similar to those of the Vapourer in size and general form but the colours are different. They are mainly blackish on their bodies and the main tufts of hair are more of a brownish-orange. There are also yellowish hairs and white, yellow and orange markings. After spinning their cocoons the larvae turn into curious yellow and black striped pupae that look a bit like the bodies of wasps. Is this colouration an effort to deter possible predators? Like The Vapourer, the caterpillars eat a very wide range of food-plants, including Docks and Sorrel species (*Rumex*), Rosebay Willowherb (*Chamerion angustifolium*), and trees including Oaks, Alder and Blackthorn.

Yet another moth species with a female that is unable to fly is the Winter Moth (*Operophtera brumata*). As its name suggests it has the unusual habit of flying in the winter months and can be found between October and January. The male is a brownish colour and flies by night searching for the females of its species, which climb up tree trunks after hatching from pupae that were buried in the ground. After mating they lay their eggs on the bark and on twigs. The eggs hatch in spring just as the trees are coming into bud. The caterpillars are "looper" caterpillars, called this because of how they move along with a loop being made of the body as the back part moves to follow the head. In America, caterpillars like this are known as "inchworms," which is another apt description, because they look as if they are measuring the ground they are walking on, and in this species the larvae reach about one inch in length. They are green in colour and feed on a very wide range of trees and bushes. The looper or inchworm caterpillars are a clue to the family the Winter Moth is included in. It is a member of the very big Geometer moth family, a moth family in which all species have caterpillars that loop along. Many of them also are camouflaged to resemble sticks.

Yet another moth with a looper caterpillar and a female that cannot fly is the Belted Beauty (*Lycia zonaria*). It is a very rare species only currently found in two places in north-west England and one in north Wales. In Scotland it is restricted to the west coast and the Hebrides, while in Ireland it has been found in County Antrim. This moth lives on sand dunes and salt-marshes, as well as heaths and dry grassy areas. The caterpillars feed in June and July on a variety of plants, including Common Bird's-foot Trefoil (*Lotus corniculatus*), Kidney Vetch (*Anthyllis vulneraria*), clovers (*Trifolium spp.*), Yarrow or Milfoil (*Achillea millefolium*), Creeping Willow (*Salix repens*), Burnet Rose (*Rosa pimpinellifolia*), as well as Yellow Iris (*Iris pseudacorus*). These larvae are coloured a brownish-grey or greenish and have single yellow lines along their bodies. The pupae are formed buried in the ground. The male moth is attractively patterned with bands of dark and white or light grey, he has a fluffy thorax and feathered antennae. The female, like the other moths females that are unable to fly, looks more like a hairy grub, although she does have rudimentary but useless wings. The male Belted Beauty flies by day and night in March and April. After mating, the female lays her eggs amongst vegetation and they are said to be able to survive inundation of water if in a salt-marsh. Threats to this species are mainly coastal development, and because the females do not fly, they are unable to move far to colonise new areas.

The Peppered moth has a stick caterpillar

The Peppered Moth (*Biston betularia*) deserves a chapter in this book for several reasons, the first being that it is an outstanding example of Charles Darwin's Theory of Evolution in action. It demonstrated what Darwin called Natural Selection. The Peppered Moth is usually a light greyish-white speckled with dark spots, hence the "peppered" moniker. However, in the Industrial Revolution era, large numbers of moths with sooty black wings and bodies started to appear. Known as var. *carbonaria,* they are perfect examples of Industrial Melanism. They appear to have evolved as a successful adaptation that helps the moth's survival in cities where walls, buildings, and even tree trunks, are darkened by sooty deposits from the dirty air pollution from factories. These dark-coloured moths are hard to see when resting on an equally dark background, whereas the normal pale for, var. *typica,* stands out and can easily get eaten by birds and other predators. These Peppered Moths with sooty wings became the common form in many parts of cities like London and Manchester. When steps were taken to reduce air pollution and cut down on fossil fuels being burned the normal light-coloured form became the dominant variety again.

The normal variety is difficult to see on a lichen-covered wall or trunk, and lichens only do well when the air is clean. In other words, the sooty *carbonaria* variety of the Peppered Moth was a visible guide to the condition of the air when it came to pollution by soot. Before the Industrial Revolution the dark form of the moth was very rare. The melanic variety helped its survival by camouflaging the moths. But camouflage does not end there with this species because it also has an unusual caterpillar that also successfully blends into its background. An intermediate variety also exists that is halfway between the dark and light forms and is known as var. *insularia*.

The Peppered Moth caterpillar looks like a twig, or a broken stick. It holds itself very still and erect on a branch where it is living and looks very like a natural outgrowth of a tree or bush. These caterpillars are a brownish-grey with rough skin and have tiny warts and flecks of lighter colouring to look just like lichen growing on a twig. When in motion though they reveal that they are actually a type of looper caterpillar, like some of the species described earlier on, and the moth it is the larva of, is yet another member of the Geometridae family. The Peppered Moth and its caterpillar are found in a wide range of habitats, including gardens, parks, hedgerows and woodland. The larvae feed on a very wide variety of trees and shrubs, including Apple, Birch, Blackthorn, Oaks, Hawthorn, Lime, Willow, Poplar, Blackberry, Black Currant (*Ribes nigrum*) and Hops. They can be found between July and September and they bury in the soil to pupate. The Peppered Moth is difficult to see in all stages of its life-cycle and because it has demonstrated Natural Selection and the Theory of Evolution so well, the species has even become known as "Darwin's Moth."

The Swallow-tailed Moth (*Ourapteryx sambucaria*) is also a moth in the Geometer family and it has a very thin looper caterpillar that looks just like a twig until it moves. The adult moth gets its name because its hindwings have a projection on each one, the "swallowtail," and it shares this similarity with the Swallowtail Butterfly we looked at earlier in this book. It feeds on a wide variety of trees and shrubs, including Ivy (*Hedera helix*), Blackthorn, Hawthorn, Privet (*Ligustrum ovalifolium*) and Elder (*Sambucus nigra*). This species overwinters as a hibernating caterpillar that resumes feeding in the spring. The Swallow-tailed Moth flies in July and is often seen in gardens and parks. It is a large moth that is very butterfly-like in appearance and has very pale yellow wings that are banded with two darker lines on the forewings and one similar line on each hindwing. It is still common and widely distributed. One more moth with a caterpillar that loops as it moves and mimics a stick or broken twig is the Brimstone Moth (*Opisthograptis luteolata*), and just like the Brimstone Butterfly we described at the beginning of this book, this moth gets its name because of its bright yellow wings, which in this species also have some chestnut-brown markings. The Brimstone Moth is a common species and its green or brownish caterpillars feed on Hawthorn and Blackthorn. It flies from April to October and is found in woodland, parks, gardens and where there are hedges that include its food-plants.

Many of the stick caterpillars have another trick that helps their survival in addition to looking like twigs. They can spin safety lines of silken thread on which they can hang their bodies suspended in mid-air. If such a caterpillar falls or is shaken out of where it has been living and feeding it can reel itself back by climbing up the thread. Smaller larvae are particularly good at this, and some species like the caterpillars of the Winter Moth can also travel from one tree to another whilst carried on air currents. I recall, when I was a boy, and was finding Vapourer Moth larvae on Flowering Currant bushes in my grandparents' garden, as detailed earlier on, that I also often also discovered some interesting black and white and orange looper caterpillars feeding on this plant too. They were the larvae of the Magpie Moth (*Abraxas grossulariata*), a very attractive moth with wings of white that are marked with yellow and also with many black spots. Its body is yellowish-orange and dotted with black. The reason I mention this moth, is because it was one of the first species in which I encountered a looper caterpillar, and one that could haul itself up a silken thread if dislodged from the bushes it was on. Sadly this once very common moth is yet another species that is declining today. Pesticides are most likely to blame.

Moth caterpillars that live in wood

Goat Moth. An illustration from British Entomology by John Curtis (1940s)

We usually think of caterpillars as a stage in a butterfly or moth's life-cycle in which the young insect feeds on leaves, but surprisingly there are actually moth caterpillars that feed on wood and live inside the trunks and branches of trees. The Goat Moth (*Cossus cossus*) is a good example of one of these. It is a very large moth with greyish-brown wings marked with many darker markings and white flecks that give the wings excellent camouflage when the insect is resting on the bark of a tree. This insect's wings look just like cracked bark. The very large caterpillar is a very dark red across its back with yellowish-orange sides and a shiny black head. It reaches a length of up to 10cm, and feeds inside the trunks of many types of deciduous tree, such as Oak and Ash. Because of this the Goat Moth is found in woodlands, parks, in gardens, along riverbanks, and anywhere else that there are plenty of trees.

The caterpillar lives three or four years hidden away inside the tree it is burrowing through and eating, and spends its final winter as a pupa after leaving its host tree in August or September. The Goat Moth caterpillar descends to the ground and forms a cocoon covered in soil where it stays until the following summer. The adult moth does not eat, having done all its feeding in its long life as a caterpillar. It is this caterpillar that gives the species its name Goat Moth, because this larva has a musky smell that has been likened to that of goats. The Goat Moth is a very scarce species in the UK though widely distributed, and also found in Europe, Asia and North Africa. The Goat Moth is a member of the Cossidae family, which also includes the Leopard Moth (*Zeuzera pyrina*). Like its cousin the Goat Moth, this species has a wood-boring and wood-eating caterpillar. The Leopard Moth's larva feeds inside the trunks of very many trees and the species is found in gardens, parks, and woodland. Again, like the Goat Moth, the caterpillar takes three years or more to become ready to pupate, and again the adult moths do not feed. The caterpillars change into pupae underneath the bark of host trees.

The Leopard Moth, or Wood Leopard Moth, is named after the large cat species because it is spotted all over, and it has six prominent black spots on its white, fur-covered thorax. The background colour of its wings is white too so this moth is very easy to see due to the bold and contrasting colouration. The Leopard Moth is on the wing in June and July, and sometimes as late as September. Besides being found in the UK, where it is still a fairly common species, this moth is encountered in many parts of Europe, Asia and North Africa as well. Because the caterpillars live in burrows inside the branches and trunks of trees, they can cause serious harm to smaller trees. They will feed on many species of fruit trees and also on olive trees, so in countries where fruit and olives are important crops, the Leopard Moth is often regarded as a pest, which seems a shame for such an attractive and unusual species.

Moths that disguise themselves as bees and wasps

Besides the Goat Moth and Leopard Moth, which have caterpillars that live in burrows in tree trunks and eat wood, there is a large family of moths that not only have caterpillars with a similar form of eating behaviour but also deserve a place in this book because they look more like bees and wasps than moths. The Clearwing Moths or Sesiidae, as they are known to science, are a very large family of 1370 species and 51 different genera. Most of them are found in the tropics but there are around 100 species found in Europe. So there are very many types but sadly many of them are very rare. The Clearwing Moths are a wonderful example of Batesian mimicry, a term we talked about much earlier on. They mimic other insects in the interest of their own survival and as a defence strategy. If a would-be predator sees what it believes is a wasp or bee it is far more likely to leave it alone for fear of getting stung. These strange moths have red, yellow, orange or white stripes that form rings around their bodies.

The Clearwings are aptly named too because their wings lack scales and are transparent, just like those of bees and wasp species. Another way they mimic the stinging insects is by flying by day in the sunshine. When a clearwing lands on a flower to feed on nectar it looks just like some species of bee or wasp. One of the most frequently seen clearwings in the UK is the Currant Clearwing (*Synanthedon tipuliformis*). I remember seeing these on Blackcurrant bushes in my father's garden.

The Currant Clearwing is a fairly small moth with a black body, yellow collar and two yellow lines on its thorax. Male moths have four yellow rings around the abdomen and females have only three. There is a tuft or fan of black hair at the tail-end of these moths. There is also a dark band marked with orange on the forewings of this species. The caterpillars of the Currant Clearwing feed inside the woody stems of currant bushes, and will also attack Gooseberry (*Ribes uva-crispa*) bushes. This clearwing moth can be found in allotments and gardens where currants are grown, and also in woodlands and other places that wild currants grow. The Fiery Clearwing (*Pyropteron chrysidiformis*) is similar but different. It has orange forewings, hence its "fiery" description in its name, and orange again in an otherwise black tuft of hair at the end of the abdomen. Its body is ringed with yellowish-white. The caterpillar of this clearwing feeds inside the taproots of Curled Dock (*Rumex crispus*) and Common Sorrel (*R. acetosa*). The Fiery Clearwing is rare and declining but is found at the top of shingle beaches, on cliffs and along roadsides near the sea.

The most spectacular examples of moths that mimic wasps and bees are probably the Lunar Hornet Moth (*Sesia bembeciformis*), and the very similar and closely related, Hornet Moth (*S. apiformis*). The Lunar Hornet has transparent wings and a mainly yellow abdomen ringed with black. Its thorax is black too, as is the head and antennae but there is a yellow collar as well. This moth really does look like a hornet or a wasp, and is probably often not seen by people because they think it is the stinging insect it mimics so well. The caterpillars of the Lunar Hornet Moth feed in tunnels they make in the trunks of willows, sallows and poplars. It frequents damp places, such as fens and marshes where the trees it depends on grow, and is also found in woodland, moorland, and old quarries that have become overgrown.

The slightly larger Hornet Moth has a wingspan of 38-42mm, whereas the smaller Lunar Hornet has a wingspan of 30-38mm. It can also be distinguished from the Lunar Hornet because it has a black collar and yellow patches on its head. Its abdomen is black and yellow and banded with rings just like a wasp or hornet. This species has caterpillars that feed in burrows they make in the trunks of poplar trees and often tunnel just below the bark.

Both types of hornet moth have life-cycles in which their larvae may need two winters before they emerge as adult moths in June. The Hornet Moth caterpillars pupate in cocoons beneath the bark and leave the trees at the base of the trunks of host trees. The moths can be found resting on these trees, and are found anywhere that poplars grow. Having said that, the Hornet Moth is regarded as Nationally Scarce in the UK but it is also native to Europe and the Middle East, as well as having been introduced to North America. This moth has been blamed for the dieback of poplars and regarded as a pest but not everyone is convinced about this.

Two more moths that mimic the look of bees and wasps are not clearwings but hawk-moth species. They are aptly named Bee Hawk-moths. In the UK and Europe there are two types, the Broad-bordered Bee Hawk-Moth (*Hemaris fuciformis*) and the Narrow-bordered Bee Hawk-moth (*H. tityus*). The Broad-bordered Bee Hawk-moth has a broader dark border on the outer edges of both sets of wings. These wing- borders are a dark reddish-brown that appears almost black and edges the almost transparent wings. The abdomen of this moth is covered in yellowish hair and ringed in the middle with two black bands next to each other. It has black antennae that are clubbed.

The Broad-bordered Bee Hawk-moth flies from May to June and is found in woodland and wooded heathland where the main food-plant for its caterpillars, the Wild Honeysuckle (*Lonicera periclymenum*) grows. The moths feed while flying and hover in front of the flowers they are gathering nectar from. This species loves to feed from Honeysuckles but Bugle (*Ajuga reptans*) and many other flowering plants are acceptable. The caterpillars will also eat cultivated honeysuckles and the Snowberry (*Symphoricarpos albus*).

The Narrow-bordered Bee Hawk-moth looks very similar but, not surprisingly, it has narrow borders on its wings. This bee-hawk favours pastures, grassy places and chalk downs, all of which are suitable habitats for the Field Scabious (*Knautia arvensis*) to grow in, and it also frequents marshy heathlands and damp meadows where the Devil's-bit Scabious (*Succisa pratensis*) can be found. These are the plants this moth needs for its caterpillars. Like its cousin, the Narrow-bordered Bee Hawk-moth flies in May and June and the larvae are found after this and spend the winter as pupae. Both bee hawk-moths do a good job of disguising themselves as bumble-bees, though are a lot more agile in flight.

The Buff-tip Moth looks like a broken twig

Disguise as a twig or stick is not only employed by many species of caterpillar like those described earlier on in this book, because the Buff-tip moth (*Phalera bucephala*) does an amazing job of looking like a twig too, a twig that has broken. It holds its silvery-grey wings wrapping around its body and they have dark markings like cracks in bark. The head and thorax of the moth are a pale buff colour and the same shade of colouration is found again at the tips of the forewings. At first glance it is very easy to mistake this insect as a broken birch twig because the wings look like birch bark and the buff colouration at each end looks just like the pale wood of a tree. It holds itself very still and this helps with the deception. Even after being alarmed and taking flight it swiftly assumes its twig-like appearance as soon as it lands.

The Buff-tip is a common species and its caterpillars feed in groups on a large variety of deciduous trees, including Birch, Sallow, Willow, Oak, Hazel, Alder and Lime. The larvae are yellow and black, with hairy bodies and black shiny heads, and can be seen from July to as late as October. Often found on lime trees in city streets, because they feed in groups, they can easily leave a section of a host tree bare. The caterpillars pupate under the soil and emerge as moths the following May, June or July. Although common this species is often not seen because it flies at night and its camouflage keeps it hidden by day. The Buff-tip is a member of the Notodontidae family of moths and there are some more unusual species in this group that we will be taking a look at a bit later on here in this book.

Not a hummingbird but a hawk-moth

Many insects protect themselves by looking like another more dangerous insect or by resembling a natural object like the Buff-tip Moth does, however, some species simply look like something else because of their behaviour and having a similar appearance. There is a species of hawk-moth that is often mistaken for a hummingbird, even though it is being sighted in countries where real hummingbirds do not live. The Hummingbird Hawk-moth (*Macroglossum stellatarum*), though, is aptly named, because in flight it looks so much like the bird it is named after. This moth hovers in front of flowers it is feeding from and can move at a very fast speed, in fact, so fast that its wings are a blur and they produce an audible hum. It has a brownish-grey abdomen marked with two white spots, brown forewings and orange hindwings.

The Hummingbird Hawk-moth has a very long proboscis and specialises in gathering nectar from tubular-shaped flowers. Petunias, Jasmine, Honeysuckle (*Lonicera* spp.), Butterfly Bush (*Buddleia davidii*) and Red Valerian (*Centranthus ruber*) are all favourites. This moth has a remarkable memory too and often returns to the same flowers day after day at the same time. The Hummingbird Hawk-moth is native to southern Europe and North Africa, and is found as far east as Japan. It is a migrant moth too and a strong flier and often ends up in countries far north of where it is usually found. This moth will migrate to the UK, for example, but cannot survive the winters, though, it is thought this may alter with Climate Change. Nevertheless, it has been recorded as far north as The Orkneys and the Shetland Islands. In the UK it is usually seen between June and September with occasional specimens seen at other times in the year.

The majority of these moths seen in Britain are migrants from the south of France, but their numbers are topped up by moths that have hatched from pupae formed in the UK. The Humming Hawk-moth produces two or three generations each year, and can be found all year round, as long as it is warm enough. I first came upon these moths when I was living in Tenerife and have seen a lot here in Portugal too. The caterpillars feed on species in Rubiaceae, the bedstraw and madder family, but also on a variety of alternative food-plants, including the Red Valerian, which, as already mentioned, is also a favourite as a source of nectar for the adult moths. The caterpillars are colourful with green or reddish-brown bodies, yellow and white stripes, white dots, black tubercles and yellow-tipped blue tail spikes.

Although this moth prefers to fly in bright sunlight, it can also be seen on the wing at dawn, at dusk, and even in damp, cloudy weather. Many other species of hawk-moth are great at hovering and have long proboscises that they use for gathering their food from deep within tubular flowers but none of them are as likely to be mistaken for hummingbirds as the Hummingbird hawk-moth. One very large species that hovers and is a migrant to the UK, often seen on the south coast, is the Convolvulus Hawk-moth (Agrius convolvuli). Like its name suggests, this species has a caterpillar that feeds on Bindweed species in the Convolvulus genus. The moth has grey wings but the abdomen is prettily banded with black and pink, and a grey line down the centre. This hawk-moth is found in the Mediterranean areas as well as North Africa. It flies from June late into the autumn but is unable to survive the British winter. When hovering by Petunias and other flowers and gathering nectar with its long outstretched proboscis the Convolvulus Hawk-moth can easily remind the viewer of a hummingbird.

The Lobster Moth and Puss Moth

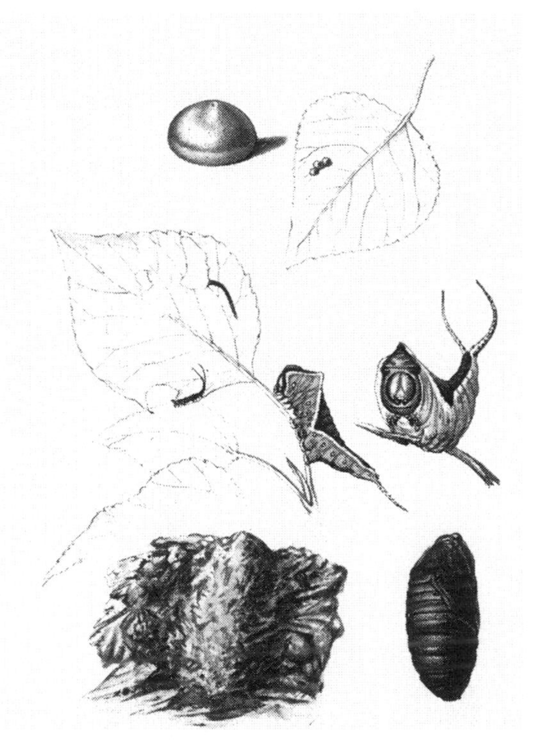

Puss Moth ova, caterpillar, cocoon and pupa. Richard South (1907)

The Lobster Moth (*Stauropus fagi*) gets included here because it is such a strange insect, well, the caterpillar certainly is. The Lobster Moth doesn't look particularly special, and nothing like a lobster, so you'll be wondering why it has this name. The caterpillar, though, is one of the strangest looking insect larvae in the world, and certainly looks similar to a crustacean. When this caterpillar first hatches out it eats only its own eggshell. The tiny insect stands guard on the remains of the eggshell, and at this stage of its life looks more like an ant or a spider than a caterpillar. It has long front-legs and appendages at its tail-end which it wriggles violently about. After the first skin-moult it becomes more like a normal caterpillar and behind eating leaves. The Lobster Moth caterpillar may have a more usual diet from now on in its life-cycle but its appearance continues to look very odd.

The caterpillar has humps on its back, a reddish-brown colouration, very long legs in front, a disproportionately large head, and then at the other end of its abdomen there is a swollen last segment that carries two long appendages. It looks almost as if it has two heads and that there are antennae where its tail should be. If the Lobster Moth caterpillar is disturbed it puts on a display by holding out its long spidery legs and holding back its true head arched over its back. The caterpillar feeds on several deciduous trees with Beech, Birch, Oak and Hazel being the usual choice in the UK. In other parts of its world range this species feeds on different trees and shrubs. It is found throughout Europe and in parts of Asia and also in Japan, where it is reported to use Wisteria as a food-plant, as well as several trees. The caterpillar spins a strong cocoon amongst dead leaves in which it pupates. The Lobster Moth adults emerge the following year from May to July. The moth is greyish-brown and quite large with a wingspan ranging from 40 to 70mm. The species is found in woodlands in southern England and south Wales in the UK. The Lobster Moth is a member of the Notodontidae family, which has some other moths with bizarre looking caterpillars.

The Puss Moth (*Cerura vinula*) is as striking as the Lobster Moth when it comes to having unusual looking caterpillars. In this species the caterpillar is mainly an apple-green colour but with a dark purplish-black saddle on its back. The head is circled with red and yellow and has a black dot on each side so that it looks like a face looking at you. At the end of the abdomen are two appendages that stick upwards and when alarmed are able to protrude pink-coloured filaments. The black saddle is edged with yellow making the caterpillar a very colourful and attractive insect. If disturbed the Puss Moth caterpillar will raise its head whilst extending the filaments from the tail appendages and waving them about. If this fails to deter a potential predator the insect is able to squirt formic acid as well in its defence. Even when young they look very weird because they are a dark blackish colour and have the two appendages at the end of their abdomens, which contain the extendable pinkish-red filaments. These filaments are as long as the length of the bodies of the tiny caterpillars and can be held back over the body area.

The young larvae also have a projection on each side of the head that looks like ears. These unusual caterpillars grow large and feed on Poplars, Aspen, Willows and Sallows. The caterpillars spin a tough cocoon made with chewed-up wood chips and attach this to a tree trunk or wooden post where it is camouflaged and blends in because it looks like wood and is made from wood. This species gets its name from the adult moth, which is greyish-white with darker markings and very fluffy, hence, the Puss Moth's supposed likeness to a cat. The males have feathered antennae too. This moth flies from May to July, and the larvae are found from July to September. The Puss Moth is fairly common and is found in parks, gardens, scrubland and woods, anywhere really where the trees it needs can be found growing. Like the caterpillar of the Lobster Moth, that of this species makes a visual impression you are not likely to forget. As well as the Puss Moth there are Kitten Moths. Not surprisingly, judging by the name "kitten," these species are like smaller versions of the Puss Moth. The Poplar Kitten (*Furcula bifida*) has a caterpillar that looks like a small Puss Moth caterpillar, and as the moth's name suggests it feeds on Poplars, including the Aspen. The Sallow Kitten (*F. furcula*) has a larva that feeds on Sallow, but also on Willows and Aspen. This species is smaller than the Poplar Kitten.

Finally there is the Alder Kitten (*F. bicuspis*). As its name suggests, the caterpillar eats the leaves of the Alder, though it is also found on the Birch. This kitten moth can be distinguished from the other kitten moths, not only by its choice of food-plant but because the adult moth has the most contrasting appearance with a dark slate-grey band across the centre of its whitish forewings, which it folds over its abdomen. A locally distributed moth, it is found in woodland areas where Alder and Birch grow. The Lobster Moth, The Puss Moth and the three species of Kitten Moths are all examples of members of the Notodontidae, a family of moths that includes many species with very unusual caterpillars, although the moths are usually not very colourful. The English group name for this family is the Prominents. This is because many species have a tuft of hair on each forewing which results in a tuft that sticks upwards from the wings when the moth is at rest. The tuft is "prominent." I like to think that the bizarre appearance of some of the larvae of moths in this family make them prominent in another way too.

Butterfly Gardening

Now that I have given you plenty of examples of the weird and wonderful lives of many species of butterfly and moth, I hope you would like to discover more about what you can do personally to help these amazing creatures. One of the best ways, if you have a garden or access to one, is to do some butterfly gardening. In other words, making your patch of land attractive to butterflies and moths. By doing so, you not only help in the survival and conservation of these insects but bring a touch of magic into your garden, where you can see that magic at work. Let us take a look at what a good butterfly garden needs.

Butterflies need food for the adult flying insects and this comes usually in the form of nectar from flowers, and they also need a supply of foodplants for the females to lay their eggs on and the resulting caterpillars to be able to eat. Some butterflies will sip the juices from fermenting fruit in autumn too but it is the flowers you grow that will make the most impact when it comes to attracting butterflies.

The same goes for moths too, although there are a surprising number, some of which I have written about in this work, that do not eat at all as adults. Nevertheless the majority feed by gathering nectar from flowers just like butterflies. The only main difference being that most moths do so at night and the butterflies are the day-crew. So what are some of the best flowers to grow in a garden for butterflies and moths?

The Butterfly Bush or Buddleia (*Buddleia davidii*) is highly recommended for attracting both butterflies and moths. I remember when a white variety of this shrub in my parents' garden used to have an incredible amount of butterflies on it. For example, there might be four Small Tortoiseshells, three Small Whites, three Large Whites, two Peacocks, a Comma and a Painted Lady all at the same time. This was in Cardiff, that was long ago in the 1960s, and since then most species have declined drastically, but this bush is still an excellent way of attracting any butterflies that might be around where you live. It has long spikes of purple, lilac, pink or white flowers that are highly perfumed. The Butterfly Bush is very hardy and fast growing and can shoot up several metres in a year. Prune it back and it will sprout vigorously. A wide mixture of colourful flowers is a good way of attracting butterflies and moths, as well as bees and all the other pollinating insects.

Some other plants I personally recommend are Cosmos (*Cosmos bipinnatus*), Purpletop Vervain (*Verbena bonariensis*), Ice Plant (*Sedum spectabile*), Lavender (*Lavandula* spp.), Wild Marjoram/Oregano (*Origanum vulgare*), Zinnia (*Zinnia elegans*), Michaelmas Daisy (*Aster amellus*), and Globe Thistle (*Echinops* spp.). Grow any or all of those and you should see butterflies and moths feeding from them. You have a selection of short plants like the Ice Plant, Lavender, Wild Marjoram and Michaelmas Daisy along with much taller ones like the Cosmos and Zinnia. The Globe Thistle is perennial and clump-forming and tall. It will come back year after year delighting with its blue and spiky globe flowers that bumblebees and honeybees love just as much as the butterflies do. Ice Plant and Michaelmas daisy put on a show until late in season and attract the autumn butterflies. You can expect Small Tortoiseshells and Peacocks on these.

Speaking of butterflies in the autumn, if you have an Apple or Pear tree, leave some windfalls to ferment. Some butterflies like the Red Admiral and Comma are partial to fallen fruit. If you have any Ivy (*Hedera helix*) growing on a wall or up a tree, let it grow big enough to flower. This is one of the last flowering plants to provide nectar for the last butterflies still flying, which are usually Red Admirals. It is a wonderful plant for a butterfly or wildlife garden for other reasons too. The Ivy is a foodplant for the caterpillar of the delightful Holly Blue (*Celastrina argiolus*), as well as some interesting moth caterpillars, such as the Swallowtail Moth. The Holly Blue gets its name from the Holly (*Ilex aquifolium*) tree, which is its choice of food for its caterpillars in spring, but then for the late summer brood it switches to the Ivy. Grow both the Holly and the Ivy to attract this little butterfly, and for the evergreen foliage. The foliage of these plants, especially the Ivy, provide a dry place for insects to find shelter in the winter months. Having a wild part of the garden is another wonderful idea. Even just leaving an area where grass can grow as it pleases can be a help to several butterfly species. The Meadow Brown (*Maniola jurtina*), Gatekeeper (*Pyronia tithonus*), and Speckled Wood (*Pararge aegeria*) are just three of the butterfly species from the "Browns," or the Satyridae family, which need long grass as food for their caterpillars.

Many people do not realise that there are many butterflies that need grass to survive. Mowing lawns for gardens and parks, as well as roadside verges, destroys the food for many caterpillars. Growing wildflowers, either by letting whatever germinates naturally, or by giving the project a hand by sowing a wildflower mix, is sure to benefit some species.

Speaking of wildflowers, the Stinging Nettle is a wildflower, though sadly many people think of it as a weed. Growing a patch of Nettles is an excellent way to attract butterflies and moths. Already mentioned elsewhere in my book, I pointed out that the Small Tortoiseshell, Peacock, Red Admiral, Painted Lady and Comma are the British butterflies that use nettles as a foodplant, and the main foodplant for the first three of these species. There are many moths that have larvae that feed on nettles too. One of these is the Snout Moth (*Hypena proboscidalis*), which gets its name because of its snout-like projection between its antennae. The Small Magpie Moth (*Anania hortulata*), as would be expected judging by its name, is "small." It is also black and white but is not related to the other Magpie Moth detailed elsewhere in this book. A pretty little moth, it is a member of the Pyralidae. Its caterpillar feeds in a rolled up leaf of the Stinging Nettle or will also eat Woundwort (*Stachys* spp.) and bindweeds (*Convolvulus* spp.).

If you would like to be really adventurous, you might consider growing either of the Buckthorns to potentially attract the Brimstone Butterfly, which we talked about towards the beginning of this work. Speaking of shrubs and trees to grow, if you have room for a willow or even a poplar, you are likely to get many moth caterpillars. Two common species that are very large and spectacular are the Poplar Hawk-moth (*Laothoe populi*) and the Eyed Hawk-moth (*Smerinthus ocelluta*). The first of these moths has brown and greyish-brown scalloped wings that look like dead leaves. It holds the wings in an unusual posture with the forewings pointing downwards and the hindwings held further forward in a more horizontal position. The hindwings can flash an orange-red patch if the moth is disturbed. This species of hawk-moth does not feed as an adult but its large and vibrant green caterpillars do a lot of eating and feed on the foliage of poplars and willows. The Eyed Hawk-moth is somewhat similar but its hindwings have pink patches with blue eyespots on them, hence its name. Like the Poplar Hawk, it flashes its hindwings if alarmed. The caterpillar of this species feeds on poplars, willows, and also Apple trees. It is often found in gardens. The two hawk-moths can hybridise and this sometimes happens in the wild producing a moth more similar to the Eyed Hawk-moth parent. These moths will find the trees they need if you have them in your garden.

My father used to leave a poplar in his back garden because every year there were hawk-moth caterpillars on it. I once grew a Sallow in my back garden and ended up with Poplar Hawk-moth larvae on it several years in a row. Getting back to talking about butterflies, in the same garden, I had Painted Lady caterpillars on the Hollyhocks (*Alcea rosea*), Small Tortoiseshell and Red Admiral on the Stinging Nettle patch, Comma larvae on the Gooseberry bushes, and Small and Large White caterpillars on the Nasturtiums (*Tropaeolum majus*). Hollyhocks and Nasturtiums are both excellent examples of showy garden flowers that are also a useful part of any butterfly garden. Many gardeners complain about the damage the white butterfly caterpillars do to their carefully grown cabbage, broccoli, sprouts and cauliflowers but the Nasturtium is an alternative source of food. It grows quickly and will cover a large area of ground, so you can easily end up with enough for the caterpillars and still enjoy its colourful flowers and rounded leaves. Actually, although the whites have been long detested by gardeners, even these species have declined in numbers so perhaps could do with a helping hand from keen butterfly gardeners.

Another area of the garden that can be used to attract butterflies and to support a small local colony is the lawn. Common Bird's-foot-Trefoil (*Lotus corniculatus*) is a food source for the caterpillars of the Common Blue (*Polyommatus icarus*). This plant will grow in a lawn that is not cut too short, and it is possible to mow around the patches of this pretty wildflower. The males of this little butterfly are blue, as their name suggests, and the females are mainly brown. This is a butterfly that will live in gardens if its food-plant grows there. I remember seeing them in the cul-de-sac street I lived in for many years in the Ely suburb of Cardiff. The main reason was that there was a neighbour at the end of my block that had a large front-garden lawn, and in it, you've guessed, were patches of Bird's-foot-Trefoil.

If you grow Holly and Ivy, you could also have the Holly Blue in your butterfly garden. Two wildflowers you might like to try growing to specifically attract the Orange-tip Butterfly (*Anthocharis cardamines*) are the Garlic Mustard (*Alliaria petiolata*) and the Lady's Smock or Cuckooflower (*Cardamine pratensis*). The males of this species, which are on the wing in late spring from April onward, have bright orange tips to their forewings, and green mottling on the undersides of the hindwings. The females look more like Small White butterflies unless you see them up close when their hindwings on the underside can be seen to be mottled with green. The females also have black tips to their forewings, which adds to the visual similarity to the Small White. This is a butterfly of hedgerows, wood margins, meadows, churchyards and gardens. The main plants the female Orange-tips are seeking are Garlic Mustard, which has white flowers, smells and tastes like garlic, and grows by hedges, along roads and on the banks of ditches, and the Cuckooflower, which has pale lilac-pink or mauve flowers that it carries above the grass of the damp meadows and grassy places it grows in.

The Orange-tip is a good example of a butterfly that you might see in your neighbourhood and fancy having a go at attracting it to your garden. Growing the right food-plants is a good way of trying to do this. The caterpillars are interesting because they are an unusual example of a cannibalistic larva. This species has caterpillars that will eat one another if they encounter each other. They are long and thin and green so they look very much like the stalks of the plants they are on. The chrysalises they turn into continue the camouflage means of deception because they look just like thorns. They have a sharp point and stick outwards from the stem they are attached to. The Orange-tip chrysalis has this method of protection but otherwise it survives exposed to whatever the elements bring. This chrysalis that looks like a thorn has no protection from the cold, the rain or wind. Yet survive they do and emerge as butterflies the following spring.

I have already mentioned how grass that is allowed to grow long can attract some butterfly species. There are two fairly common Skipper butterflies that come into this category. The Small Skipper (*Thymelicus sylvestris*) and the Large Skipper (*Ochlodes sylvanus*) are the species I am thinking of. The caterpillars of both butterflies will feed on the Cock's-foot Grass (*Dactylis glomerata*), and the larvae of the Small Skipper are often found on Yorkshire-fog (*Holcus lanatus*). Both these skippers are pretty little insects with orange-brown wings. The Large Skipper is larger and also has flecks of lighter orange on its wings. Both butterflies are very fast flyers and seldom remain still for long but they will perch on a flower while sipping nectar. The Large Skipper tends to prefer staying at the edges of fields and by hedges than the Small Skipper which will venture out into the middle of a field. The Large Skipper can often be seen feeding on the flowers of the Blackberry, and this is an excellent plant for attracting butterflies of many species. You can also enjoy the fruit it yields as well. The Small Skipper flies from June to August, and the Large Skipper can be on the wing a bit earlier, flying from May to August. It is possible to encounter both species at the same time. There are several other skipper butterflies but the Small and Large are the most likely ones that you will see, and that can be attracted into a garden if you leave a part where the grass can grow.

After Dark

The butterflies and day-flying moths can be seen in the sunshine but we mustn't forget the nocturnal moths. After dark a whole new world comes alive in the garden and in the countryside. This is a world well worth exploring, and you will be amazed by what is out there hidden under the cover of darkness. If you have a Butterfly Bush take a look at it at night. A torch or flashlight will reveal what representatives of the night crew have come to feed on the copious nectar. You may be surprised to find even more moths on this bush than the butterflies you see on it by day. Species from the Noctuid moths are one of the main families with species that like to feed from the Buddleia.

I have told you about the butterflies that I remember seeing on the bush in my parents' garden but now let's take a look at the moths I used to find there after dark. The Large Yellow Underwing (*Noctua pronuba*), Silver-Y (*Autographa gamma*), Cabbage Moth (*Mamestra brassicae*), Dot Moth (*Melanchra persicariae*), Dark Arches (*Apamea monoglypha*), Gothic (*Naenia typica*), Flame Shoulder (*Ochropleura plecta*), Bright-line Brown-eye (*Lacanobia oleracea*), and Heart and Dart (*Agrotis exclamationis*) were some of the regulars. The names of these moths are magical enough for me. From the Geometridae, I could expect the Swallowtail Moth, Brimstone, Garden Carpet (*Xanthorhoe fluctuata*), Willow Beauty (*Peribatodes rhomboidaria*) and V-Moth (*Macaria wauaria*).

This last species was once common but in recent years has become increasingly rare. The moths were so intent on feeding on the sweet nectar that they didn't mind the torch being shone on them. Sometimes the intricately beautiful Buff Arches (*Habrosyne pyritoides*) would make an appearance. This moth has grey-brown wings patterned with orange-brown arches and zigzags and white lines edging some of the markings. It is a very pretty creature with the patterning of its wings looking very artistic. This species was easily found on the railway bank behind where my parents' house was and used to mainly stay there but sometimes, they would fly over the back wall. There were plenty of brambles on the bank and that is the plant the caterpillar of the Buff Arches eats. Recent studies have shown that this moth is one of many that has suffered badly from the effects of increased light pollution. This is a moth that likes it to be really dark after dark.

As I have already mentioned the Buff Arches is a moth that used to mainly be found on the railway bank alongside the back lane of the family house, and this brings me to another great way of looking to see what you can find after dark. It is a method of attracting moths that is known to enthusiasts as "treacling" or "sugaring." These names are very apt because the would-be moth spotter prepares a sugary mixture that may well contain treacle, and then they paint this in strips on walls, posts, tree trunks and other places that moths might well be flying past.

The aim is to attract the nocturnal insects away from natural sources of nectar and instead to lure them to feast on the very sweet concoction you have made. I used to do a spot of treacling in the back lane and that is how I know that the Buff Arches could be more easily found in that location. Treacling suggests that treacle is an important ingredient, and indeed Fowler's Black Treacle, was a basic. I haven't seen it around for a long time so I'm not sure if it is still available but it used to be on sale in most grocery stores. It was used for making black treacle toffee, treacle tart and other sweet confections. Besides treacle, molasses and sugar, other ingredients can be added, including a dash of alcoholic spirit, such as rum or brandy. Experienced treaclers have their own recipes. You go along half an hour or so after you have painted your sticky bait to see what has been attracted by the bait. Besides moths you can expect to find other insects, such as earwigs, but on a good night many a local moth will be there greedily feasting and oblivious. It is exciting seeing what does turn up.

Using a light-trap is yet another way of attracting moths in your area or at a location in the countryside. This method is used by professional lepidopterists surveying the distribution and population of moth species. There are several types of light-trap. The Heath Trap is the cheapest, easily portable and can be packed away flat. It consists of a collapsible box, a funnel, and a light. The Skinner Trap is bigger, more expensive, collapsible too, and has a slot entrance for the insects but sometimes moths escape from this variety of trap. The Robinson Trap is a large round, plastic container. It is the most efficient of the different types, and there is no escape, however, the downside is that it is the most expensive. It is also bulky and doesn't collapse. Traps employ high-powered light bulbs. Mercury Vapour bulbs are probably the best and were very popular. They are apparently banned by the EU, though still available elsewhere. Actinic and fluorescent tube lights are also used. The purpose of whatever trap is to attract moths so they can be identified, counted, and then released. These traps are harmless, and actually help scientists understand how well the various species are actually doing. Sadly, none of the methods of studying moths at night brings anywhere near the results you could expect in the past. It is to be hoped that this decline can be reversed, and I hope this book will go some way to helping to achieve this. When studying moths you can discover the magic of the world at night as well as by day.

And Finally

And finally, I would like to leave you with some organisations and a lepidopterist I can personally recommend If you would like to take another step into finding out about butterflies and moths. I do hope that the magic of these insects has inspired you to do so.

The first is Butterfly Conservation. The name Butterfly Conservation only has "Butterfly" in it but moths are just as important and the organisation wants to see "A world where butterflies and moths thrive and can be enjoyed by everyone, forever."

Registered Office: Manor Yard, East Lulworth, Wareham, Dorset, BH20 5QP
Website: https://butterfly-conservation.org/
Email: info@butterfly-conservation.org

The second is Buglife, which proudly says of itself: "Buglife is the only organisation in Europe devoted to the conservation of all invertebrates." Besides butterflies and moths, Buglife are just as concerned about spiders and other arachnids, crustaceans, slugs and snails, worms and all other creeping, crawling, or even slithering along, creatures without backbones. Find out more at their main website: https://www.buglife.org.uk/

Worldwide Butterflies (WWB) has been going for over 50 years. I bought stick insects and exotic silkmoth eggs and pupae from them when I was a boy. The company has been a part of my journey of discovery and I am glad to see they are still going strong today. WWB stocks an amazing variety of captive bred species of butterflies and moths, including many rare species. They offer special deals on species like the Garden Tiger Moth and Small Tortoiseshell Butterfly for anyone who wants to have a go at helping bring back these once common species into their area. WWB also stocks books, cages and containers, light-traps and living plants that are used by various caterpillars. The website is a mine of information too. They deliver in the UK and Europe, as well as elsewhere at the customer's own risk. https://www.wwb.co.uk/

I would call Bart Coppens an expert when it comes to butterflies and moths. He has devoted much of his life to studying these insects and rearing them in captivity. Check him out on YouTube where you will find many hours of fascinating videos in which he shows you many of the insects he cares for, as well as taking the viewer out spotting butterflies in the Netherlands where he lives. Bart has the distinction of being the only person in the world who reared a particular African tiger moth species from egg through to adult and documented the life-cycle of the species. Bart, like myself, was clearly captivated by the magic of butterflies and moths when he was a boy too. Here is his website: https://breedingbutterflies.com/

Books I consulted while researching for this one:

Maravalhas, E. (Editor), *as borboletas de portugal* (*the butterflies of portugal*), Stenstrup, Denmark, 2003

Randle, Z. Evans-Hill, L.J., Parsons, M.S., Tyner, A., Bourn, N.A.D., Davis, A.M., Dennis, E.B., O'Donnell, M., Prescott, T., Tordoff, G.M., & Fox, R., *Atlas Of Britain & Ireland's Larger Moths*, Pisces Publications, Newbury, 2019

Tolman, T. & Lewington, R., *Collins Butterfly Guide*, HarperCollins, London, 2009

PAGANISM & SHAMANISM

What is Paganism? A religion, a spirituality, an alternative belief system, nature worship? You can find support for all these definitions (and many more) in dictionaries, encyclopaedias, and text books of religion, but subscribe to any one and the truth will evade you. Above all Paganism is a creative pursuit, an encounter with reality, an exploration of meaning and an expression of the soul. Druids, Heathens, Wiccans and others, all contribute their insights and literary riches to the Pagan tradition. Moon Books invites you to begin or to deepen your own encounter, right here, right now.

If you have enjoyed this book, why not tell other readers by posting a review on your preferred book site.

Other *Magic of* titles you may enjoy...

The Magic of Cats

Your Purrfect guide to the magic of cats in this world and the other

Andrew Anderson

978-1-80341-066-1 (Paperback)

978-1-80341-067-8 (e-book)

~~~~~~~~~~~~~~~~~~~~~~~~~~~~~~~~

The Magic of Serpents

A remnant from the age of the dinosaur, the serpent was originally a symbol of arcane knowledge from the old gods.

Scott Irvine

978 1 80341 056 2 (Paperback)

978-1-80341-057-9 (e-book)
~~~~~~~~~~~~~~~~~~~~~~~~~~~~~~~~